THIS BOOK WAS WRITTEN BY

D1527478

Your full name is

_____

_____

_____

_____

_____

Your job is

_____

_____

_____

_____

_____

Your eyes
are

_____

_____

_____

_____

_____

Your favorite food is

_____

_____

_____

_____

_____

Your favorite drink is

_____

_____

_____

_____

_____

Your favorite sport is

_____

_____

_____

_____

_____

Your favorite movie is

_____

_____

_____

_____

_____

Your favorite song is

_____

_____

_____

_____

_____

Your favorite TV show is

_____

_____

_____

_____

_____

Your favorite animal is

_____

_____

_____

_____

_____

Your favorite
dessert is

_____

_____

_____

_____

_____

Your favorite color is

_____

_____

_____

_____

_____

Your hero
is

_____

_____

_____

_____

_____

Your favorite team is

Your favorite thing to wear is

_____

_____

_____

_____

_____

Your favorite thing to do is

_____

_____

_____

_____

_____

Your favorite place at home is

_____

_____

_____

_____

_____

Your favorite game to play is

_____

_____

_____

_____

_____

Your favorite way to relax is

_____

_____

_____

_____

_____

If you could be an animal you would be

_____

_____

_____

_____

_____

You deserve
an award for

_____

_____

_____

_____

_____

You smell like

_____

_____

_____

_____

_____

You are more handsome than

_____

_____

_____

_____

_____

You like to go to

_____

_____

_____

_____

_____

You are not very good at

_____

_____

_____

_____

_____

You are as strong as

_____

_____

_____

_____

_____

Your favorite holiday is

_____

_____

_____

_____

_____

Your favorite vacation place is

_____

_____

_____

_____

_____

You act silly when you

_____

_____

_____

_____

_____

Your talent is

_____

_____

_____

_____

_____

Your best
friends is

_____

_____

_____

_____

_____

You love it when

_____

_____

_____

_____

_____

Your favorite restaurant is

_____

_____

_____

_____

_____

You always smile when

_____

_____

_____

_____

_____

You always say

_____

_____

_____

_____

_____

You are really good at fixing

_____

_____

_____

_____

_____

You get mad when

_____

_____

_____

_____

_____

You are really good at

_____

_____

_____

_____

_____

You are smart because you know

_____

_____

_____

_____

_____

You never

You always laugh when

_____

_____

_____

_____

_____

Your favorite story to tell is

_____

_____

_____

_____

_____

Your favorite thing that we do together is

_____

_____

_____

_____

_____

You are funny when

_____

_____

_____

_____

_____

You don't
like to

_____

_____

_____

_____

_____

You are the happiest when

_____

_____

_____

_____

_____

You call me

_____

_____

_____

_____

_____

You are
scared of

_____

_____

_____

_____

_____

You always tell me that

_____

_____

_____

_____

_____

You know how to

_____

_____

_____

_____

_____

You taught me to

_____

_____

_____

_____

_____

You always
help me with

_____

_____

_____

_____

_____

You always forget to

_____

_____

_____

_____

_____

You don't like it when I

_____

_____

_____

_____

_____

You are happy when I

_____

_____

_____

_____

_____

You are proud of me when I

_____

_____

_____

_____

_____

The thing that makes you happy when you are sad is

_____

_____

_____

_____

_____

The best thing about you is

_____

_____

_____

_____

_____

You are special because

_____

_____

_____

_____

_____

I love you because

_____

_____

_____

_____

_____

You and I

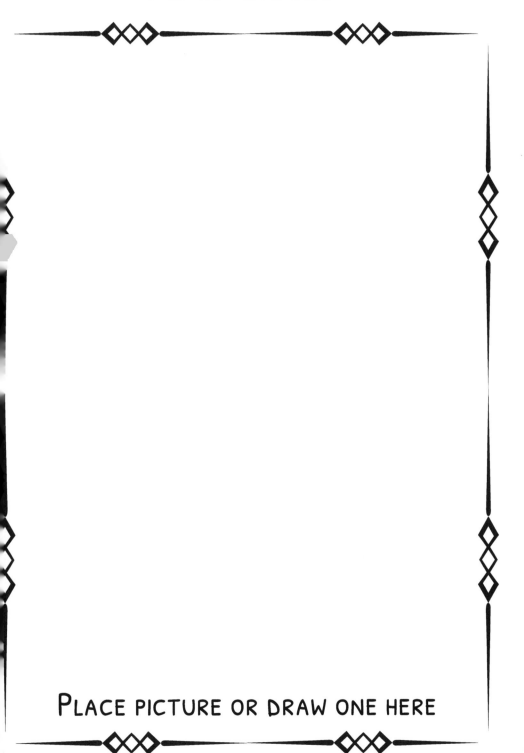

PLACE PICTURE OR DRAW ONE HERE

Made in the USA
Columbia, SC
15 June 2021